THE GIRLFRIEND'S
CODE OF ETHICS

THE GIRLFRIEND'S CODE OF ETHICS

Hope Bakari, M.Ed
Tonya Sherman, M.Ed
Lauren Lewis, M.Ed

iUniverse, Inc.
New York Lincoln Shanghai

The Girlfriend's Code of Ethics

iUniverse books may be ordered through booksellers or by contacting:

iUniverse
2021 Pine Lake Road, Suite 100
Lincoln, NE 68512
www.iuniverse.com
1-800-Authors (1-800-288-4677)

Because of the dynamic nature of the Internet, any Web addresses or links contained in this book may have changed since publication and may no longer be valid.

The views expressed in this work are solely those of the author and do not necessarily reflect the views of the publisher, and the publisher hereby disclaims any responsibility for them.

Front Cover Photo by Tonya Sherman; All other photos by Eric Johnson.

ISBN: 978-0-595-45783-0 (pbk)
ISBN: 978-0-595-70304-3 (cloth)
ISBN: 978-0-595-90085-5 (ebk)

Printed in the United States of America

This book is dedicated to Wanda, the secretary at work, the so-called nurse, and all the other women who need a code of ethic to live by.

Contents

Introduction

GIRLFRIEND! What in the hell were you thinking? You know you were wrong! No matter how hard you try to convince yourself that what you did was right, you know it wasn't cool. So, why is it that we're having this conversation again? You know the rules! Or, do you?

What if you were presented with the opportunity to get to know a tall, dark and handsome hunk of a man who you happened to meet at a party, would you jump at that opportunity? What if your girlfriend had her sights on the same man? What would you do then? Then, to add a little twist of drama to the mix, let's say your girlfriend had begun communicating by telephone with Mr. Tall, Dark and Handsome a few weeks before the party, but because of work, school, death in the family, or some other reason, was unable to attend. Now you're there, girlfriend's not, and the two of you hit it off before you realize that your catch is the same fish your girlfriend just gloated about hooking. Damn!! Just like Murphy's Law to come in and mess with your chance at romance. But, what do you do?

Do you decide he's off limits and move on to your next victim? Or, do you gleefully prance off into the moonlight with Mr. Handsome, conveniently forgetting any mention of "what's her name" and her desire to make it happen with your newly acquired man?

As much as we might feel unfairly victimized when we are labeled ruthless in our pursuit of "the one," we unfortunately continue to make choices that prove our disregard for one another as women, as sisters and as fellow members of the "universal clit." Our actions have destroyed families, interfered with our professional lives, broken hearts, severed friendships, and created an atmosphere of cynicism that somehow continues to perpetuate this madness.

Whatever happened to the once recognized pact between girlfriends, anyway? How do we so easily move from "Girl, I've got your back" to "Bitch, I've just picked out the perfect knife to stab you in the back"? For some reason, dissing each other seems to come as naturally as doing our hair and nails and without any regard for rightness. But, what is rightness? Sure enough, we all have our own sense of right and wrong that is shaped by our own personal experiences, but justifying what really amounts to selfishness to make us feel good about the mess we do is wrong, and all these wrongs are weakening the connections we long for, need, want, and claim we are proud of in a girlfriend-girlfriend relationship.

By the way, who is your girlfriend anyway? For one, your girlfriend is not limited to those people with whom you share some sort of tie, like your best friend, your soror, your classmate, your sister. These close relationships make saying No to Mr. Handsome slightly more doable. But, remember this. Your girlfriend is also the cashier at the local grocery store. She is the divorced, single mother of three who you see dining at TGIFridays. Your girlfriend is also the wife of the man you may be eyeing or, even worse, screwing. Your girlfriend is your daughter, your mother, and your grandmother. Your girlfriend is YOU every time you look in a mirror.

Considering this, you would think that we all would feel the same way about the strength of our bond. We are, or at least should be, on the same team—a part of the same club. And we are. ALL women are members of the club of the "universal clit"—the combined influence of chromosomes, genes, experience, and history that make women the same. You would think that this "universal clit" would be all that was needed in order for us to keep our allegiance to one another intact, shielding us, hopefully, against the possibility of drama. You would think that by nature of our familiarity we would sincerely think on what it is we want to be judged. You would also think it unnecessary to put into writing codes of ethics that are seemingly common sense and have always, theoretically, been present in the first place. But, our actions consistently prove that we are in need of a common set of written rules that guide us when we are unsure about the "rightness" or "wrongness" of what we have done, are doing, or are about to do. Let's face it girls! We have gotten out of hand! We have bought into this male-shortage garbage and have decided that no female is off limits—not sister, not mother, not best friend and definitely not the woman down the street whose name we don't know.

Now, this book is not for the hard core "do wrong because I don't care what you think" girl or the "I'm gonna get mine, so screw you and your mother too" girl. This book is for those of us who really want to do the right thing by the rest of us. This book is for that girlfriend who has either grown tired of hurting other women or just doesn't want to risk "going there." There being that point of no return where you do something that you may regret for-ever—that point where you wish someone had dragged you aside and talked some sense into you. So ladies, here we go with 51 rules for us to follow and a little 911 on the spot emergency advice to help you on your way. We call them the Girlfriend's Code of Ethics.

CHAPTER 1

The Myth of the Vanishing Man

Oh where, Oh where, have all the good men gone? Oh where, Oh where can they be? Snap out of it women!! That sad song has gotten old! All you need to do is head straight to the nearest mall, church, bookstore, restaurant, post office or right under your very own nose working in the office or cubicle next to yours. Good, single men are every-where!! So, let's first dismiss the notion that there is some sort of phenomenon that is causing our men to simply disappear (poof!) into thin air. Regardless of what we have told ourselves, they are not all married, jailed, on drugs, or gay.

Of 100 women polled, 85 percent stated that they believe a shortage of men exists in the United States. But, here is something to think about. The United States Census Bureau reports that there are approximately 94 million men between the ages of 18 and 64 living in the United States. Of these 94 million men, 52 percent or 48 million are married, 2 million or 2.8 percent are reportedly gay or bisexual, and approximately 2 million are incarcerated. This leaves a grand total of approximately 42 million single, heterosexual men in the United States *alone*. Granted, not all of these men are suitable for dating. That is a given, just as not all women are suitable for dating for a number of reasons. But, why are we tripping? Why are we desperate? Why are we so intent on sharing men when we might think twice about sharing a slice of pizza, or a bite of a chocolate bar? Some have said, specifically, that there is a shortage of "good" men in America, with an emphasis on "good." The question is, then, what are we looking for? What is our definition of good?

When defining "good," several words come to mind. Honest. Committed. Loving. Intelligent. Hardworking. Caring. Who wouldn't want a man that possessed these qualities? But, what about words like tall, handsome, educated or wealthy? Suddenly, the pool of available and desirable men begins to vanish. And, just as suddenly, we women begin to act as if our lives and our ability to breathe depend on being attached romantically to a man. With this desperation comes the behavior that many of us have come to despise, putting men in the position of feeling like they are some sort of rare commodity. We meet Mr. Tall, Dark and Handsome, fall for him, find out he's married or has a girlfriend, and some of us just don't care. Some of us believe that we will never get another chance at love if we let this unavailable, and dishonest, man go. When instead, we should do a Beyonce, point him towards "the left," and wait, because "in a minute" another man will be on his way.

In reflecting on song lyrics and other creative outlets, there are so many that promote man-sharing and woman on woman "fight to the death over a man" behavior that we have begun to think of it as normal. But, there are also just as many that address female empowerment and girlfriend stick-togetherness. These are the messages that we should look to for guidance when we have man-stealing on our minds. Really, all we need to do is simply believe that we are deserving of a good, positive relationship with one of the millions of good, positive men that exist in our world, and silence that voice that continues to scream that *"all of the good men are gone."* Tell that negative voice inside to just shut up, so you can get on with the business of finding that husband or boyfriend or lover you really want and, even more importantly, deserve.

Scenario:

Camille is a woman who thrives on the attention she gets from men. She feels especially thrilled when that man is taken. As a result, she has repeatedly been the other woman in a series of relationships. She has benefited in a number of ways, from having her rent paid regularly, to receiving expensive gifts. And, if this is not enough, Camille makes her presence known by calling the wives of her married lovers, intentionally "forgetting" her belongings in their vehicles, befriending their children and generally causing as much chaos as she can. When another girlfriend asks her to explain her motivation for constantly becoming involved with married men, she explains that good men are hard to find so, therefore, she could care less that the men whom she approaches are taken. She, according to her, is going to take what she can get, and if that means taking another woman's man, then so be it.

Code #1

Never buy into the male shortage misconception. **No matter what we think or what we are told, there is NO shortage of men on this planet. Remember, according to the United States Census Bureau, there are approximately 42 million unattached, heterosexual men between the ages of 18 and 64 from whom we may choose.**

Girlfriend 911: Avoid having tunnel vision in your quest for the ideal mate. Look beyond those criteria that you have set for yourself—the job he should have, the car he should drive, the money he should make, the race he should be, his height, his eye color—all of those charac-

teristics that mean absolutely nothing and only serve to limit your possible dating pool.

Scenario:

Doretha recently divorced and has been very depressed. Marie tells Doretha that she knows someone who can help her overcome her depression and cheer her up. She goes on to tell her that the man is happily married (supposedly), has no intentions of leaving his family, but simply wants to have a fling on the side. Though Doretha gets upset by this offer, Marie continues to push the possibility of the two hooking up.

Code #2:

Never introduce your girlfriend to a married man with the intention of having them hook up romantically. **First off, this is irrational behavior on Marie's part. She is willing to step on another girlfriend's toes (the man's wife) to supposedly make her friend happy, but will possibly set her girlfriend up for more heartache and pain.**

Girlfriend 911: Avoid imposing your values, or lack thereof, on someone else. Regardless of actions, we all know it is wrong to become involved romantically with someone who is married. Therefore, don't pretend that it's okay for you or your friend to engage in this behavior.

If you want to introduce your friend to someone, find someone single that may be compatible with her. And, while you're at it, find someone single for yourself as well.

Scenario:

Missy has been physically attracted to Matthew for several years. The problem for Missy is that Matthew has been happily married and committed to his wife, Laura, for fifteen years. Despite this, Missy has propositioned Matthew repeatedly over the course of many years. Matthew, though, has persistently refused her advances. Finally, Missy decides to take matters into her own hands and contacts Laura. Missy lies to Laura, and tells her that she has been having an affair with Matthew for ten years. Missy's lie is just enough to cause Laura to question her marriage and her husband's commitment.

Code #3:

Never be so desperate as to lie to a woman (or to yourself for that matter) about having a relationship with her significant other. This is the case of a woman who is in need of some serious counseling.

Girlfriend 911: Instead of wasting time concocting stories about someone else's man, use the time to either find an available man of your own, or seek counseling to learn why you would be so fixated on one that you would go to any length to snare him.

Scenario:

Your girlfriend invites you out for happy hour in order to meet her new male companion. At some point during the evening, your girlfriend excuses herself to the restroom. While she's gone, you slip her friend a note with your name, number and the words "call me" written on it. When she returns, you behave as though nothing ever happened.

Code #4:

Never pursue a man in whom you know your girlfriend is interested.

Girlfriend 911: Ding Dong!!! You're at Happy Hour damnit!!! Happy Hour usually equates to a room full of working men having a drink after work. So, how about leaving your girlfriend alone with her friend so she can get to know him for herself? In the meantime, strike up a conversation with one of the other men there and pass your "call me" note on to him.

Scenario:

For eight months, Sonya has been in a very satisfying relationship with Rico. The sex is the bomb and she has no problem sharing intimate details about their sexual escapades with her girlfriends. Christine, one of Sonya's girlfriends, begins to think about Rico and often fantasizes about having sex with him in many of the ways that Sonya has described.

Code #5:

Never fantasize about your girlfriend's man. It is said, "So a man (or woman in this case) thinketh, so is he (or she)." In other words, if you obsess too heavily about screwing your friend's man, eventually you may try and make it happen. PLEASE, STOP THE MADNESS!!!!!

Girlfriend 911: Find someone untouchable or unattached in order to fantasize about. Matthew McConaughey and Will Smith are great options. You can even keep a huge poster of your object of desire near your bed. This way, you won't risk the chance of doing something regrettable, and, even worse, unforgivable.

Code #6:

Never repeatedly give intimate details about your man to your girlfriend. Otherwise, she runs the risk of breaking code #5.

Scenario:

Tasha and Veronica work together as elementary school teachers. They have always been cordial, but have never developed a relationship beyond the workplace. One afternoon, while both Tasha and Veronica are in the main office, Veronica's brother stops in the office to drop something off to her. Tasha, seeing how attractive Veronica's brother is, immediately begins to talk to Veronica about the possibility of them hanging out together sometime.

Code # 7:

Never befriend a woman simply to gain access to her man, her brother, her father etc. **Though it is normally a very obvious ploy, it happens** *all of the time.* **Unfortunately, this move goes all the way back to our days in grade school when we would have crushes on our friends' brothers.**

Girlfriend 911: Don't you think it's time for us to grow up and handle our business like adults?

Scenario:

While shopping, Vanessa meets Charles, a handsome and soon to be married young man. They hook up for what initially is supposed to be a one-night stand, but turns into two nights and then three. Two weeks before he is supposed to marry his fiancé, Charles calls off the wedding with the intention of now being in a relationship with Vanessa. Vanessa accepts this arrangement with open arms and proceeds to begin a full blown relationship with Charles.

Code #8:

Never sleep with a man knowing he's engaged to someone else.

Girlfriend 911: Like we said, there are 42 million single men from whom you may choose. Pick one of the 42 million that is unattached and uncommitted, and leave this one alone.

Code #9:

Never assume a man is going to be faithful to you if he ends a serious relationship with someone else in order to be with you. **No woman's "stuff" is so good to a man that he doesn't think he can find some just as good somewhere else.**

Girlfriend 911: Beauty, money, and all the sexual favors in the world will never keep a man. If it is in the man's nature to stray, then he will. So, it is up to you to respect yourself and treat yourself like the precious jewel that you are.

Scenario:

Three girlfriends and two male co-workers go on a business trip together. Girlfriend number one becomes interested in male co-worker number one. Girlfriend number two says that male co-worker number one is off limits because he is intimately involved with girlfriend number four (at home). Girlfriend number one says, "Whatever! She isn't here!" and becomes involved with male co-worker number one anyway, even after being warned.

Code # 10:

Never disregard a direct warning to steer clear of a man who is already involved in a relationship. You risk the chance of severing not just one friendship, but two, or even three.

Scenario:

Cynthia has applied for a position as a social worker at a local community center. Her first interview is with Mr. Ledford, the director of the center. Initially, the interview is completely professional. Eventually though, Mr. Ledford begins asking Cynthia her personal opinion about issues he has with his wife. He also speaks openly about how attracted he is to her and how he hopes they can meet for drinks sometime. Cynthia later tells her friend Portia about her "interview" and includes the "stuff" Mr. Ledford said about his wife.

Code #11:

Never believe, and especially repeat, the negative stories told to you by a man about his wife. If in the same breath a man is dogging his wife out and asking you out on a date, he isn't worth the time anyway.

Girlfriend 911: Can you spell S-E-X-U-A-L H-A-R-R-A-S-M-E-N-T?

Breaking the Code
Beware of the Babysitter

"I was very eager to enroll my daughter in day care and soon made an appointment at a school nearby. I had only been in town for about two months and had heard that this was one of the best day care centers in the area. I noticed that one of the teacher aides was very friendly and talkative. Each day, Brenda would greet me with a smile and a question about my personal life. I spoke with her freely because I had no friends in the area and welcomed her company and conversation. About three weeks after my daughter started at the day care, I received a phone call from Brenda stating that she was ending her employment at the day care center, but would be willing to continue as my daughter's caretaker at her home for a discounted price. I refused her offer, but did agree to allow her to sit for us on the weekends. The babysitting, lunch dates and girl talk continued until we developed what I thought was a genuine friendship.

Two years into the friendship, I received a telephone call from her husband, Bill, stating that my husband, Allen, was having an affair with Brenda. I immediately told my husband about the conversation and we both had a huge laugh about it. Brenda was so unlike someone I thought Allen would be interested in that I completely ignored the call and assumed it was only a prank.

A week or two later, Brenda knocked on my door to tell me that it was all true and that she was, indeed, having an affair with my husband. She expressed how she thought I needed to leave him because I was too good for him and could do much better. When she didn't get the response she wanted—my departure—she became angry. At this point, I simply asked her to leave my home. She began making harassing phone calls, leaving crude messages on the answering machine and attempting to come over many times to bring gifts. She would call me at home and at work. Brenda knew the layout of my home, the contents of my closet and other details she had not been privy to simply through my relationship with her. In addition, her harassing behavior usually took place following business trips where I may have to be out of town for a day or more. When confronted, Allen admitted to the affair, but assured me that he had ended the relationship and that it had been "nothing" from the beginning.

For me, life went back to normal until the day that Brenda pulled up behind my car in the driveway of my home, got out of the car and proceeded to tell me again how awful Allen was and how I was too good for him. When I asked her to leave, she called me a nigger and said that I was a stupid bitch. All of this took place while my children watched. When Allen arrived, I forced him to call the police, and we filed a report and a restraining order. As soon as the restraining order expired, she began harassing me again. It became so terrible that I began warning the people I knew that if anything happened to me then she had something to do with it. I lived in constant fear for my life and the lives of my children.

This drama continued for five years and all the while my husband was still involved with her! It only ended when he found another eager home wrecker and I had finally had enough."

Lavonya M., 33

Breaking the Code
Tit for Tat

"Ronald and I began our relationship as friends and though attracted to one another, things remained that way for a long time. We had been together as lovers for several months before I became suspicious about his behavior. Often, when I would accompany him to business-related functions, a woman he referred to as an "old friend" and freely talked about, would be present. Her name was Sherry, and she looked every bit the tramp she turned out to be. I really don't remember what triggered my sudden distrust. I do know that I learned how sneaky a woman can be when she needs to be. I began searching his caller I.D. I even figured out the code to his cell phone voicemail and would listen daily to the messages that she would leave him. Through listening to her messages it was clear to me that she was aware of and accepted the relationship that I had with him. She seemed to think of it as a game, making references to pleasing him sexually in a way that I could not or directing him to call her when I had left. The entire experience was crazy considering the length of time I remained in the relationship even after learning about his indiscretions. It seemed to develop into some sort of sick competition where my goal would be to spend as much time with him as possible, which, in my mind, would ensure that this was time not spent with her."

Tiffany E., 37

Breaking the Code
Extra Credit

"I was very sad to hear that I would be leaving all of my friends in Houston and moving to Portland, Oregon where my husband had received a professorship at a major university. I was sad with the realization that I would be by myself—without friends—to support me in raising my two children. My husband promised that I wouldn't have to work and this motivation helped create a more positive outlook regarding the move. After recently finishing several weeks of marriage counseling, the move also symbolized an opportunity for us to start anew as a couple.

Once we arrived, everything was great. We settled into our new routine and I began doing volunteer work for various community centers. My husband received the department head position soon after he started his new job, which translated into more time spent away from home. His responsibilities included working closely with several graduate students, one in particular.

Life went along smoothly until I received a frantic telephone call from my husband stating that he was packing his office because he had just lost his job. Once he got home, my husband informed me that he was being sued for sexual harassment. He went on to say that the graduate assistant that he had been supervising for the past few months was making these accusations. After an hour of probing, my husband admitted to sleeping with this woman—once.

The girl's lawsuit began with the attorneys first questioning me about my husband's whereabouts on certain days and times. Throughout this investigation, I found out that the graduate student stated that she and my husband had been involved for six months and that she had received credit hours that she had not earned legitimately. I learned later that this student had gone to several parties and bragged about how she was actively setting up a certain professor—my husband. Also, unbeknownst to me, that girl even volunteered at one of the community centers at which I volunteered. She even went to lunch with a group of us one day. What in the hell was that about? I was afraid for months because I never knew if I was going to turn on the T.V. and see all of this mess on the news. This shit went on for years!! Years!! I stood by my husband's side throughout the trial, and he won—but not because he was innocent, but because of his professional position, and the lies I told to help protect him and my family. For her trouble, she received a small sum of money and the satisfaction of knowing that she had ruined him."

Felecia S., 28

CHAPTER 2

I Must Be Doing Something You're Not

Dear _____,

This is not a letter of congratulations on your fake wedding date. While you're walking down the aisle, your flower petals will already be dead and decayed because you stink and your actions have been foul. Each step you take will represent the pain you have caused so many. While you're standing and listening to your vows, this message should ring in your ears.

Everyone always wants to say that it's all about the kids, but today it's all about mom. You walked in on my hard work, my love, my support, and eighteen years of prayers. Do you even know who you're saying "I do" to? You don't know him. Where were you when he had to make decisions about his education and his future? You were not there making sure he survived as a student. You were not there when he was depressed and wanted to commit suicide because of bad decisions made at work. You were not there each time we went out with all of our friends and each dinner engagement with his parents. The man you met is a man who was loved by many, but especially me. The man you met was lying to you and to me. The man you met has it together on the surface, but inside is a little boy who *still* needs help.

You see dollar signs as security. You see the white picket fence and the key that turns into the fabulous home that you have never known before. Washington, D.C., Chicago, Hawaii, and Atlanta will never be enough to satisfy you and to keep him. His heart will forever long for what he left behind, for you are simply the forth on a list of pointless pussy he was chasing. Remember you said to me that you must be doing something I wasn't doing? I told you then that the only thing you were doing was screwing a dirty dick and taking a man away from his family. You excitedly shouted that he was putting you through school. Well, why didn't you come educated and ready to go instead of needing *my* husband to "put you through school"?

When you pick out your wedding dress and tacky bridesmaid gowns, I want you to know that for one year I rearranged food in my refrigerator to give it the appearance of being full. My freezer was never used because there was never enough money to buy food that would last for more than a day. Once, when a friend of ours bought food for us, my daughter went to the refrigerator, saw all of the food, and said she thought that she was dreaming. So, as you can see, while your children were benefiting from my ex's money, his own offspring was doing without. I want you to remember that. Not that you really care, but I want you to remember that what you did ruined a family. But, don't think for one second that you have it made, because you don't.

If you're wondering if I wrote him, I didn't because I don't have to. His letter is written on the lines of your face, and each time he looks at you, he will be reminded of the family he left behind and what he, and you, did to destroy it.

Sincerely,

The Ex Wife
Aka Happy and Moving Forward

❦   ❦   ❦

Scenario:

Cynthia is involved in an affair with Mark, a married co-worker. Though it is obvious that Mark is being unfaithful to his wife, he states to Cynthia that he loves his wife and family and is not going to leave them. Cynthia decides to take matters into her own hands and sends an anonymous letter to the wife, revealing the affair and other intimate details. Cynthia states in the letter that she simply cares about the wife and wants to protect her.

Code # 12:

Never call, write or otherwise contact the wife or girl-friend of the man with whom you are cheating, even under the pretense of protecting her. This is a ploy used in hopes of creating some conflict between the wife or girl-friend and her significant other. Though you will create conflict, you, more than likely, will not achieve what you had hoped. In fact, you may find that your attached lover will actually be angry with you for causing additional chaos on the home front.

Girlfriend 911: If you decide to blow the whistle on your lover, be prepared to walk in the shoes of the woman you just dissed.

Scenario:

Lloyd has a one night stand with Lisa, an old classmate from high school. Three months later, Lloyd bumps into another classmate, Michelle, and begins a serious court-ship. Lisa is a good friend of Michelle's younger sister. Lisa continues to call Lloyd and ask him out. Lloyd tells Lisa that he is currently involved with Michelle and is committed to the relationship. Lisa's response is "So! She's not in my circle! Can I see you tonight?"

Code #13:

Never attempt to hook up with a man who states to you, point blank, that he is involved in a committed relationship with another woman, particularly with one whom you have this close a connection. **Again, you risk the chance of severing a friendship with the woman's sister, as well being labeled a "ho" by the man you are so intent on screwing.**

Scenario:

After ten years of marriage, Sharon and Harold begin experiencing difficulties in their relationship. As a result, Harold becomes romantically involved with Patrice, one of the secretaries at his law firm. One evening, after Harold returns home from a "business trip," Sharon "finds" a woman's wallet in his duffle bag. The identification inside belongs to Patrice M., the secretary. Knowing who she is, Sharon proceeds to call Patrice and question her about the relationship she has with her husband. During their conversation, Patrice states that apparently Harold is with her because she must be doing something that Sharon is not.

Code #14:

Never resort to using the played out line "I must be doing something that you're not!" Of course there *is* some truth to the statement, because what you *are* doing is sleeping with someone else's man. This is wrong anyway you slice it, so stifle the ego and always remember, "What goes around comes around, everyday of the week."

Girlfriend 911: Humility is always a key element when you are wrong. In other words, don't become angry with a wife for confronting you about having an affair with her husband. Wouldn't you do the same thing if someone was sleeping with *your* husband?

Scenario:

Craig and Jennifer have dated exclusively for two years. Jennifer leaves town to begin a college prep program in another city. Mia, who has been in competition with Jennifer for years, chases after Craig and purposely gets pregnant.

Code #15:

Never forget that the choices you make, good or bad, ultimately affect those close to you. Purposely bringing a child in the world in order to win out over another woman is a selfish act that fails to consider how the drama will later unfold. **Girlfriend 911: Remember, the sins of the mother fall on her offspring as well.**

Scenario:

Brenda hires Eugene, a contractor, to complete some work on her house. Brenda and Eugene communicate back and forth several times regarding the purchase of materials. A few weeks later, Brenda receives several calls from Eugene's cell phone. When she returns the call, Tameka, Eugene's wife answers. Tameka questions Brenda regarding the purpose of the communication between her and her husband. Brenda is sensitive to Tameka's concerns so, therefore, clarifies the nature of their relationship, and even invites her to be there while Eugene completes the work. Despite this, Tameka contacts Brenda on two other occasions. Brenda finally tells her that she will find someone else to complete the work for her.

Code #16:

Never harass another woman who merely has a professional relationship with your mate. **Having questions or concerns is okay. Continuing to push the issue airs your dirty laundry, illustrates your own insecurities/paranoia, and violates the other (innocent) woman's privacy.**

Girlfriend 911: First of all, respect and accept the nature of your man's profession. If you're genuinely concerned, find a clever way to involve yourself in your husband's job. For example, if your man is a photographer, become his assistant. If he is an attorney, surprise him with breakfast or lunch. Sometimes, these actions may even protect him from his own gullibility.

Scenario:

Rhonda and Dwayne have been dating for about a year. Rhonda confides in her friend Sheila about the ups and downs of her relationship with Dwayne. She asks Sheila to speak with Dwayne in hopes that she can communicate her love to him. Rather than support her girlfriend, Sheila takes this opportunity to criticize Rhonda, and reveal some of her most personal secrets. Soon, Dwayne and Sheila begin an intimate, and secret, relationship. Three months pass before Rhonda learns about Sheila and Dwayne's undercover love affair.

Code #17:

Never use your girlfriend's pain to connect to her man in order to develop an intimate/sexual relationship with him. The essence of friendship is loyalty. You cannot consider yourself a friend if you cannot be trusted with another person's innermost thoughts and feelings. If someone trusts you enough to share details about themselves, be trustworthy enough not to use this information to your advantage.

Girlfriend 911: We often know in advance when we are about to slip into the "I don't care what she thinks" mode. When you feel this coming on, be a real friend and become magically unavailable for her or her boyfriend.

Code #18:

Never divulge your girlfriend's secrets to anyone, let alone her man. By definition, information we choose not to share with others falls under the category of secrets. If your girlfriend shares something with you that she considers confidential, reflect back on the time you felt betrayed when someone told one of your secrets or, even worse, read your diary or journal without permission. Even if your intent is not to go behind your girlfriend's back and use her secret to your advantage, keep your girlfriend's business to yourself.

Girlfriend 911: Listen to your girlfriend with a sincere heart and resist any urge to befriend her man. If the secret your girlfriend tells you is so juicy that you just have to fight like mad in order to keep it to yourself, write yourself a letter describing all the juicy details, including names, places and positions if necessary—all the *stuff* you might have to keep to yourself if you were talking to a "real" person. When you're done reading, re-reading and reading it again, tear it up, burn it, or flush it down the toilet. Just get rid of it, along with any temptation you may have to tell someone else.

Scenario:

Daniel invites Jamillah, the other woman, to the home he shares with his wife and family. His family is out of town visiting relatives. After a while, Jamillah and Daniel have sex on the bed that Daniel and his wife share.

Code #19:

Never have sex with the married man with whom you are having an affair in the house he shares with his family.
    Girlfriend 911: Damn! Must we tell you everything!!?

Scenario:

Paul has made plans to attend his family reunion with his wife and kids. He also invites Jan, who he has been secretively having an affair with for the past two years. Jan eagerly accepts.

Or

Carlos is a physical education teacher at a local high school. After working very closely with his new co-worker, Wilemina, they soon develop an intimate/sexual relationship. They have even found time to "hook up" sexually in the locker room, in their offices, and even behind the bleachers. On several occasions, the members of the physical education department have socialized at Carlos' house. Wilemina is always present and often chit chats with Carlos' wife.

Code #20:

Never spend time in the presence of your married lover's family. **It is bad enough to have that relationship in the first place. Don't make matters worse by flaunting your indiscretions in front of his unsuspecting and innocent family.**

Scenario:

Terry bumps into an old high school sweetheart who is now married with two children. They reconnect and soon become physically and emotionally intimate. He is enjoying their relationship, but has no plans to leave his family. Terry begins to suggest that she could make him happier than his wife.

Code # 21:

Never encourage a man to leave his family. **Enough said.**

Scenario:

Six months ago, Lara and Charles divorced, ending an 8 year long relationship. Charles soon remarries and has a child with his new wife, Sarah. Because Charles and Lara have children together also, they communicate often and have managed to remain close. So close, in fact, that they occasionally meet specifically to have sex.

Code #22:

Never believe that it is your right to maintain a physical relationship with a now married, or otherwise committed, Ex. **The prefix, ex, means no longer true. So, in relationships that are "no longer true," every aspect of that relationship falls under that category. It is no longer true that you are physically intimate with that person. It is no longer true that you communicate in a suggestive fashion with that person. It is no longer true that you cook for them, shop for them or mow their grass.... or, even worse, let them mow yours.**

Breaking the Code
Choices

"In my mind, my marriage was good. Not perfect, mind you, but good. I trusted my husband. I thought we were friends. I felt blessed, and I thanked God everyday for blessing me with a good man and beautiful children. I thought we were happy. I thought this right up until the time I pulled the handwritten letter out of my mailbox informing me that another woman had been sleeping with my husband for the last three years of our 13 year marriage. My initial reaction was complete denial. In fact, I refused to even entertain the possibility that it could be true. I mean, I knew this man, or so I thought. I felt he was incapable of doing something that would cut my heart into shreds. Just impossible, I kept saying to myself. Not only that, I trusted him completely.... I trusted him completely ... I trusted him.

When confronted, of course he denied everything. He reassured me that it was simply not true, that he never heard of this person, that someone must have put this letter in the wrong mailbox. But, my gut knew something that my head was trying to dissuade me from believing. There was something about the letter, and his behavior was very strange. I kept playing and replaying the words contained in the letter like a tape recorder that refused to shut off. The woman in the letter had said that she was not only sleeping with my husband, but she knew my children as well. It took me two days to figure out that if I really wanted to know the truth, I needed to ask my children. So I did just that. One day, when he got out of the car to pump the gas, I turned to my two children, Jabari, 4 and Ayanna, 2 and asked them if they had ever been to Twyla's house with Daddy. "Yesssss," my babies answered while staring at me innocently with two sets of beautiful brown eyes. My heart ached as I gasped for air. I couldn't breathe. I couldn't think. The pain I was feeling was so intense, so sharp, so crushing, I simply wanted to disappear. Run. Hide. Scream. I grabbed my chest and pressed down upon my pounding heart. I felt it beating wildly under the pressure of my trembling palm. I wanted to disappear, and I wanted to be away from him. It felt like a part of my essence died right there, in front of that gas station, in the passenger side of our Ford Expedition. Yes. Ladies and Gentlemen, at exactly 8:05 a.m., the innocent spirit of Deborah Lamont passed quietly away, and I have never been quite the same. It was amazing to me then, and still now in reflection, how I could be dying inside and no one around me even knew. "I am dying and no one knows," I kept repeating to myself. I'm dying. "Keep breathing," I reminded myself. "No one can see my pain.....breathe.... no one has to know.....breathe.... keep breathing.

I didn't understand. The last three years of our marriage had been one big, awful, painful lie. She knew he was married with kids. By her own admission she knew it, and slept with him anyway. What I have never been able to wrap my head around was how two people could have such a total disregard for the pain that they would cause someone else by sleeping together. Was there ever a point that either one of them gave any thought of me? Why was there so little regard for my heart and so much focus on the selfish desires of theirs? I don't understand. I just don't get it. What I do know is that it came down to making a choice. When a person decides to disregard marriage and commitment in pursuit of immediate gratification it comes down to making a choice. You choose to cross the line. You choose to sleep with a man despite the fact that he's married. You make the choice to forever change the way in which your spouse will look at herself, her marriage, other women, and men. YOU make the choice. It is a choice that YOU make. A choice."

Deborah L., 35

Breaking the Code
The Secretary at Work

"One of the worst things about my husband's infidelity was the feeling that everyone around me was privy to the punch line of an inside joke of which only I was left out. As a result, I never knew when interacting with one of his female friends whether there was something that I should be guarding myself against or whether I should maintain a heightened level of awareness that would help me be less of a fool in these situations. In the end, I still felt foolish and betrayed by, not only my husband, but by the women with whom he had these relationships. They were always so intent on making sure that I knew—that it was in my face, as though I deserved some level of punishment simply for existing.

On one occasion, I received a letter in the mail addressed from a man stating that his girlfriend was having an affair with my husband. In the letter, it told who the girlfriend was—a woman my husband always referred to as "the secretary at work," the neighborhood in which she lived, as well as her telephone number and details describing the circumstances under which they would meet. i.e. when he was supposed to be somewhere else. Reading this letter sent me into an automatic frenzy. Initially, I didn't say anything to my husband about the letter that I had received. I simply used the time as an opportunity to see what I could find out for myself. So, when he left the house, I would often pack up my infant son and drive through the vicinity in which "the secretary at work" supposedly lived. Sometimes, I would go to the location that he claimed to be headed just to see if he or his car was there. I spent countless hours just driving around rehearsing the scene I planned on creating when I finally knocked on the bitch's door. Eventually, I received a telephone call and another letter from the boyfriend. This letter explained that if I needed further proof of the affair he could arrange a three-way call in which I could listen in on a conversation between my husband and his girlfriend. I immediately considered this possibility suspicious. How could he arrange this without his so-called girlfriend's knowledge? Though I never found out the real deal, I believe that this concocted boyfriend was simply a ploy created by her to create chaos in my marriage, forcing me to leave. When I finally confronted my husband about these accusations, he had concocted his own story which involved a jealous boyfriend going through his girlfriend's address book and calling the wives of all the men listed in order to tell these wives that each of their husbands was having an affair with his girlfriend. I became dizzy just listening to it. Anyway, the letters continued—three total—until one evening the telephone rings and Ralph, my husband, answers it. He nonchalantly handed the telephone to me—as if he did not recognize the voice on the other line. What a crock!! It turned out to be her—the secretary at work. She proceeded to tell me, with attitude, that she did not want my husband. "I don't care whether you want him," I responded, "I want to know if you are fucking him." (Silence) With that, the conversation with, and about, the secretary at work abruptly ended."

Sissy A., 28

Breaking the Code
Pretense

"Years ago, a woman took it upon herself to not only sleep with my husband, but to graciously allow me to sit for her son while she did so. Naturally, everything was done under the pretense that their relationship was strictly platonic, and I being someone who has had many platonic relationships knew that, in theory, this was very possible. But soon it became painfully obvious to me that their relationship was not as innocent as they would have me to believe. Steven would "disappear." When he'd reappear, he'd often say that he had to stop at Wanda's for some reason or another, or that Wanda didn't have a ride and he had to give her one. Wanda was so blatantly disrespectful that she often accompanied my husband home from work or called to speak to him while at home. One day, I even entered my home to find her at my stove cooking and laughing loudly with dumb dumb, aka Steven, at her side. By this time in my relationship his unfaithfulness had become such a joke that it did not even cause me to raise an eyebrow. Nonetheless, the party came to an immediate halt when I entered the room. In the end, it took years, two children, and several affairs for me to finally say goodbye to my husband and the women he brought in and out of my life."

Theresa B., 35

Breaking the Code
Secret Revealed

"I had noticed for months that my husband had become a different kind of lover. Oral sex was at its peak and our eroticism had developed a different flavor. Though the change was welcomed, I never felt comfortable with this newness, and decided to do some investigating. Within a few hours, I came across some nude photos of a particular woman. I was taken aback, not only by her nudity, but by the stark contrast with which she and I compared. She was nothing like me. She had small breasts. She was very thin. She was pale. The finding was devastating. I was very depressed and extremely hurt, but I began a mission to find out just who that girl was. I didn't have to wonder for long. One day soon afterwards, I just so happened to be in the drug store and looked up to see the face of the skinny, small-breasted woman standing right in front of me. We talked, and she said that according to him we were not together and were getting a divorce. He had convinced her that we were having problems because of my actions, and not his. Not true.

Despite the obvious drama, I made the decision to fight for my marriage, but I knew that I was going to have to deal with that girl. Immediately after the meeting in the drug store, my husband's behavior worsened—almost as though he felt he now had permission to have this affair. After a while, I called her. She stated that nothing had changed between my husband and her, that I was tripping, and that I needed to get over it! She was extremely disrespectful. To her, it didn't matter the long term repercussions for me, my children or even herself for that matter. She came across as though I was the one who was wrong. "I want you to know that you're not going to get shit out of this," she yelled. "I am going to get your man; I'm going to get all of his money, and you're not going to have anything!" Some of what she said came true. My husband and I divorced. The skinny, small-breasted bitch set her wedding date, and in doing so freed me of ten years of stress, mental anguish, and abuse. I hope she's happy, because I sure am."

Cynthia T., 56

Breaking the Code
Hater-aide

"I finally got the nerve to call her house. I held onto the number for about a month after suspecting my husband, Jamal, was having another affair. Jamal had recently been transferred to a new city for work and only came home on the weekends. We had two school-aged children and our plan was to move the entire family there with him at the end of the school year. What changed all that was a sudden urge to clean Jamal's overnight bag. I found her wallet, and for the first time I was able to see her ugly, no credential having face up close and personal. Once again, I was shocked at my husband's choices. Another piece of shit I thought. The first time I tried to call her I blocked our number, but there was no answer. So, I unblocked the number and dialed it again. She answered on the first ring. I apologized for calling and introduced myself, Mrs. Jamal Jones. She said, "Yeah?" Just like that. "Yeah?" I really wasn't surprised by the ghettoness of her tone, nor her dialect. It was just like my husband to dig to the bottom of the barrel to find pussy. I asked her how she knew my husband, and she responded by asking me why I wanted to know. I told her that we were married and that I was planning to move to Tennessee very soon to be with him. I then told her that no matter what he has told her, we were not separated. She responded that she did not care and that she was in a relationship with him and that was all that mattered. "How does it feel to be with a married man?" I asked her. She said, "What do you think?" "I don't know," I answered, "because I've never been involved with someone else's husband." I asked her if she realized that she was not only interfering with his ability to be a husband, but a father as well. She had the nerve to say that what was important to her was that he had bought her a car and that they had an apartment and would be living together soon. I held the phone in disbelief reflecting on her confidence in describing what she was doing. She went on to say that she met him at a meeting and decided to go after him. She decided, married or not, that she was going to do whatever she had to do to make him, my husband, her man.

Shortly afterwards, I received a call from a gentleman introducing himself as her recently divorced ex-husband. I found out later that she had been married as well, and her husband had hired a private investigator to confirm suspicions he had about his wife's behavior. Once confirmed, he pursued his divorce at that point—she had been cheating on him for years, had three children by three different men and had been married three times, so she obviously had no appreciation for marriage and commitment. She even left her children with their stepfather so that she could go after my husband. I made the decision to pursue a divorce as well, not to give her what she wanted, but to close a chapter in my life that had brought nothing but misery and the

possibility of AIDS. Even though she has succeeded in living with my ex, it has not been enough—she constantly interferes in his relationship with his children and refuses to allow him to co-parent them. She's an insecure hater!"
Rachele J., 40

Breaking the Code
A Man of the Cloth

"After all of this time I still laugh a little, but grimace a lot when I think of how I once thought I would be protected from drama by having a relationship with and loving a "man of the cloth"—a minister. He had spent time with my family, as well as my son. He even had a picture of my son and me in his bedroom. It was amazing how quickly he denied us when temptation called. My telephone rang and I could hear his voice on the other end, but he was talking to someone other than me. I heard the voice of a woman asking if he had enjoyed what they had just experienced. The voice asked whether the positions were pleasing and whether they could try something different *next time*. The voice even asked about the picture of me and my son and we suddenly became the family of a good friend of his—not the woman he had been involved with for two years or the young boy he had taken to the movies just three days before. I was pissed at him. Really pissed!!! But, that voice belonged to another woman—someone like me. Why in

the world did she feel the need to call me so I could hear all of that?"
Sydney T., 26

CHAPTER 3

Being Stupid, Making Excuses, and Never Having to Say You're Sorry

Stupid! That's what it is. Just, plain stupid! Or, maybe denial is a more suitable term to describe that behavior in which you make a conscious choice to behave in a way contrary to the principles of loyalty and decency, but when confronted, you blame that behavior on something outside of yourself like alcohol, drugs, ignorance or even another woman. Often, we simply act without thinking, going on about our lives without any real thought to how our actions may be perceived by another. Other times, we unintentionally put our own girlfriends in positions that may encourage a relationship to develop between our man and them. Because we women are so sensitive to another woman's actions toward the man with whom we are trying to build a relationship, whether he is boyfriend or husband, we badly need those women who interact with our men to be just as sensitive to our feelings as they would want us to be toward theirs. Yes. It is always hard to own up to those decisions we make that result in the betrayal of one's trust, but life becomes so much more rewarding when we learn to accept our mistakes and see them as stepping stones to a drama-free life. The lesson here is for you to simply think. *Think* before you act. *Think* before you speak. And definitely *think* before you pick up the phone to call your girlfriend's man.

Scenario:

Every Friday, a few friends get together and go to happy hour. Katarina spots Billy across the bar and makes eye-contact. Billy responds by ordering Katarina one drink that eventually turns into several more drinks and conversation. They both begin to talk about their marriages. They leave the bar together, stumble to Katarina's car, climb into the backseat and proceed to have unprotected sex right there in the parking lot.

Code #23:

Never use alcohol as an excuse for screwing another woman's husband. **Even though alcohol reduces one's inhibitions, there is still a point along the way when you** know that you are losing it. This is the time when you need to get out of the situation immediately.

Girlfriend 911: Always have another girlfriend with you when you are going out drinking or having a good time. This friend can be your voice of reason when you are too intoxicated to listen to your own.

Scenario:

Jesus and Maria have been together for thirteen years. Over the years, Maria has found phone numbers, greeting cards, letters and even a vibrator in his gym bag. Eventually, Maria gets the nerve to call one of the numbers and Elida answers, surprised that Maria has called her. Maria simply asks Elida if she would explain the nature of the relationship with her husband. Elida does, and explains that according to Jesus, he and his wife had an open relationship which allowed them to have "friends" outside of their marriage. Elida repeatedly tells Maria that she is sorry for sleeping with her husband.

Code #24:

Never, ever think "sorry" is enough to make up for your wrongdoings. When we wrong someone else, an apology is always necessary, but it is only the beginning in an often long road to healing. Saying "I'm sorry" unfortunately doesn't erase what you have done to cause a person pain.

Girlfriend 911: Before becoming intimately involved with a man, do your homework. Google him. Do a background check. Visit him at home. Hell, *call* him at home—cell phones don't count. In other words, do what women do best—SNOOP!!

Scenario:

Out of the blue, Barry, Angela's ex-boyfriend, calls Samantha, Angela's close friend, in order to wish her a happy birthday. They talk briefly, wish each other well, and hang up. Samantha never tells Angela about the call.

Code #25:

Never "forget" to inform your girlfriend if her boyfriend or ex-boyfriend calls you for any reason.

Girlfriend 911: Since you never really know for sure what the man's intentions are, make your intentions clear by telling her everything before she has the chance of learning it from her man or someone else later.

Scenario:

Sitting in Starbucks, Wanda runs into Ronald, her now married ex-boyfriend. They talk, reminisce and exchange numbers. The next day, Ronald calls Wanda to set up another date, this time planned, at Starbucks. Wanda agrees, they meet at Starbucks and decide to meet again another day so Wanda can visit with the pet they once shared. A couple of days later, Ronald takes the pet to Wanda's and leaves him there for the entire day.

Code #26:

Never believe that it is ever okay to "hook up" for any reason with a now married ex-boyfriend without the current wife's knowledge. Providing justification for wrongdoing does not turn a wrong move into a right move. In addition, any circumstance that requires a man to lie to his wife or girlfriend is an obvious wrong.

Scenario:

Tonya's boyfriend, Mark, owns a local barbershop. Patrice, Tonya's close friend, has a son that is in dire need of a haircut. Patrice considers whether she should call Tonya and have her ask Mark whether she can make an appointment with him, but decides to call him herself. Patrice reaches Mark, makes an appointment, and takes her son to the barbershop for a haircut. When Mark speaks with Tonya, he mentions that Patrice had come to the barbershop earlier and that he had cut her son's hair. Though Patrice and Tonya talk daily, several days pass before Patrice ever tells Tonya about her visit to the barbershop.

Code #27:

Never, under any circumstances, call, write, e-mail or SOS your girlfriend's man without first asking permission from your girlfriend explaining why this communication is necessary in the first place and why she can't communicate this information for you.

Girlfriend 911: It is always best if the girlfriend contacts her man on your behalf. This situation is even more suspicious since Patrice fails to mention the visit. Tonya is now forever suspicious of her friend.

Scenario:

Adrian runs into Vernan, her girlfriend's man, at the grocery store and asks for his help in repairing a broken faucet in her apartment. Vernan accepts, thinking that Adrian had already spoken to his girlfriend. While he is there fixing the faucet, his girlfriend calls and overhears him in the background talking.

Code # 28:

Never allow your girlfriend's man to be at your place of residence, whether it is to make repairs, cut the grass, help you move etc. without your girlfriend being present as well. If girlfriend is not present, she sure as hell better know what's up!!

Girlfriend 911: Call your girlfriend and let her know that you are in need of the services that her husband or boyfriend provides. Let her be the messenger between you and her man.

Scenario:

As a present for her friend Sandra, Nikki gives the gift of three weeks of free personal training with her husband, Michael. Sandra soon becomes possessive with Michael's time and attention. As a result, Michael backs off and begins to avoid Sandra. Sandra then starts to create lies about Michael and tell them to Nikki.

Code # 29:

Never hire your man out as a present for your girlfriend. It places both people in a position that is precarious and fails to recognize the frailty of men and woman. It's not that you don't desire to trust your man with your friend and vice-versa; it's simply that you don't want to put them in a position that might lead them both into a more tempting situation.

Girlfriend 911: The basic rule here is to simply hire someone else for jobs of this nature. Try giving a gift certificate instead.

Code #30:

Never, out of spite, do or say anything that can jeopardize your girlfriend's relationship with her man.
Girlfriend 911: GET A LIFE!!!

Scenario:

Janai's book club meets twice each month. Often, the conversation will change into a male-bashing session where one or two women lead the conversation as they discuss all of their bad relationships. With this, they are constantly stating how all men are dogs and how none of them can be trusted.

Code #31:

Never bring your own personal baggage and negativity into your girlfriend's relationship.
Girlfriend 911: Instead of focusing on your own bad experiences, use these exchanges as a way of transforming

your opinion about men. Regardless of your past, there is always hope for a better future in love.

Scenario:

MaryAnn happened to be shopping in the mall when she runs into Jack, her friend's husband. They talk briefly, say goodbye and continue on with their individual shopping. When MaryAnn speaks to her friend that evening, she never mentions that she and Jack saw each other at the mall. The next day, MaryAnn's friend calls specifically to ask her why she hadn't told her about seeing her husband in the mall the day before.

Code #32:

Never forget to inform your girlfriend if you happen to see her man out somewhere. i.e. store, restaurant, mall, highway. **Though this is not a major faux pa, situations like these may cause a friend (especially one who is a little jealous to begin with) to question your loyalty.**

Scenario:

Leslie just received a brand new pair of breasts courtesy of the local plastic surgeon. While visiting her friend's home, she decides to show off her breasts to everyone present. She even asks her friend's husband to touch them to see how real they felt.

Code # 33:

Never ask your girlfriend's man to critique your physique, especially by using his hands.

Girlfriend 911: Go to your neighborhood gym and ask one of the male personal trainers to give you his professional opinion about your new breasts, or simply ask another woman.

Scenario:

Leroy asks Shenika to braid his hair at her shop. She suggests that they go to her home instead because the atmosphere is more laid back. Leroy's girlfriend comes to pick him up and is very upset by what she sees. Leroy is sitting there, between Shenika's legs, as she finishes his hair.

Code #34:

Never cut, braid, comb or style your girlfriend's man's hair or provide any other service while he is sitting between your legs.

Girlfriend 911: Use a chair damnit!

Scenario:

Rosa is an aspiring model who wants to put together a portfolio. In selecting a photographer, she automatically thinks of Jackson, her best friend, Gabriella's, man. After she gets her pictures back, she openly shows them to Gabriella. Gabriella is shocked and angered to see that Rosa is naked in many of the photos.

Or

Rosa is out grocery shopping with her man, who is a 6'3", 220 pound personal fitness trainer/masseuse. While out, they run into her friend, Kiki. Rosa introduces Kiki to her man, who innocently gives Kiki one of his business cards. The next week, Kiki calls Rosa's man, sets up an appointment for a massage and excitedly keeps her appointment.

Code #35:

Never use the professional services of your girlfriend's man if it involves the need to reveal your body at any time.
Girlfriend 911: Use the yellow pages instead.

Scenario:

Jan is always calling Samuel to ask for advice about her relationships. Though he is married, he still makes himself available to talk to her whenever she needs him. His wife knows nothing of this "relationship."

Code #36:

Never develop a relationship, of any sort, with another woman's man without her knowledge.

Girlfriend 911: If the man who you consider a friend is married, then you must have a relationship/friendship with his wife as well. If you cannot, then you should sever any ties you have with the man.

Code #37:

Never expect your girlfriend's man to console you through problems you are having with your man. **Though this may seem innocent in the beginning, sharing creates intimacy. Intimacy between people of the opposite sex may build an attraction which can lead into dangerous territory.**

Girlfriend 911: Talk to your girlfriend instead.

Scenario:

Sybil is friends with Edward, her girlfriend's man. Edward has frequently accompanied his girlfriend to Sybil's home. He has admired her flair for decorating and openly states that he wishes his place was decorated as nicely as hers.

Sybil offers to shop for him and redecorate his bathroom and kitchen.

Code #38:

Never volunteer to do things for your girlfriend's man—PERIOD.

Girlfriend 911: It is just as easy to refer your girlfriend's man to someone else, or to provide your girlfriend with tips that she may use to help her man herself.

Scenario:

A couple of weeks ago, Makayla had some nude photos taken to add to her portfolio. Out of excitement, she takes them over to her friend's house to show her. She arrives and even though her girlfriend isn't there, her girlfriend's man is. She winds up showing the pictures to him instead. While viewing the photos they begin talking about the sexually explicit poses and how exciting it would be to have sex with a woman who looked like her.

Code #39:

Never have discussions of a sexual nature with your girlfriend's man.

Code#40:

Never view pornography with your girlfriend's man.

Code #41:

Never show a nude or very revealing photograph to another woman's man.

Girlfriend 911: If you find yourself in this situation, think of what it is that is motivating you to discuss sex with your friend's man, or show a nude photograph of yourself. This is not an innocent act and is probably motivated by your ego's desire to outdo your beloved girlfriend in some way. Why not suggest to your friend that she take some nude photos of herself to show to him. Then, they can break the last three codes themselves.

Scenario:

A group of friends are out of town hanging out. Anaya's husband, Richard, is part of the group and acts, more or less, like the group's tour guide. Anaya, however, is not present due to a prior commitment. That evening, the group is only able to acquire one hotel room. They all, including Richard, decide to sleep together in that room on the one bed provided.

Code #42:

Never share a bed with another woman's man for any reason. Avoid the appearance of impropriety at all costs, and avoid putting yourself in a position that may lead to an indiscretion.

Girlfriend 911: In this situation, the man should be made to sleep on the floor or on a cot provided by the hotel. He can also sleep in the car. What's one night of discomfort compared to a lifetime of alimony and child support?

Scenario:

Kimberly has been dating Lance for three years. For his 30th birthday, she invites her best friend, Sammie, to join them in a threesome. During the act, Kimberly notices that Lance is focusing all of his attention on Sammie and not her. Three months later, Lance continues to push the idea of the three of them hooking up again.

Code #43:

Never invite your girlfriend to have a ménage a trios with you and your man.

Girlfriend 911: If group sex is your thing, find someone who is rarely present when you're in the company of your man. Only bring them out of the closet when it's time to do your thing. This way, no emotional attachment is formed between your man and this other woman. Choose to have a ménage a trios with two men and yourself rather than the other way around. Doesn't that sound fun?

Scenario:

Tracey has a habit of discussing personal issues regarding her marriage with her best friend, Jenny. As a result, Jenny feels comfortable enough to add her two cents to the conversation. On one occasion, she states that Tracey's man is a punk and that she could do much better.

Code #44:

Never bash your girlfriend's man to her or anyone else. If she needs to vent or needs your advice, let her do all the bashing and complaining. (Rule Breaker Policy: If your girlfriend is getting badly dissed by said boyfriend, by all means, throw this one out of the window.)

Scenario:

Adrianne invites Daniel, her best friend's man, to attend the Prince concert with her and her man. The day before the show, Daniel finds out that Adrianne has also invited her friend, Sandra, to accompany them. Daniel receives an angry phone call from his girlfriend asking why he would accept such an invitation.

Code # 45:

Never make your girlfriend believe that her man is a part of a threesome when, in actuality, he is a part of a foursome.

Girlfriend 911: You are never obligated to find a date for your girlfriend, especially when it involves stabbing another girlfriend in the back in order to make it happen.

Breaking the Code
Letting Go

"I'm not sure why it started or even how. I just know when. I was sitting at dinner at Outback with Thomas, one of my college boyfriends, when the phone rang. When I answered it no one said anything. I thought it was strange, but paid no attention. It didn't cross my mind that it may be Thomas' wife. Besides, how could she get my number this quickly? It didn't matter really because I had no plans of doing anything other than having dinner with him and catching up a little. But the phone calls persisted. It didn't dawn on me until later who it was. It was Rhonda, Floyd's (my ex-boyfriend) new girlfriend. Like I said, I don't know why that woman decided that she needed to start harassing me. If she really knew me, she would have known that she was making a big mistake. But, anyway, she started it, and it got messy. Really messy. I mean the kind of mess with police, vandalized cars, drunken fits, car chases, family and friend involvement, and deep, humiliating hurt with trips out of town to "get away from it all" and to heal.

Rhonda. The funny thing was that I knew of her. Floyd had told me about her, described her, and had even driven her car to our job. So, I was cool. At least that's what I told myself. But, she started calling me and telling me to leave "her man" alone. Her man? To me, she was an outsider, an instrument wielded by Floyd. What she didn't know (or maybe she did know) was she was getting in the middle of something that had a five year history. Didn't she know that I had already relinquished the battle and moved on, or I was at least trying to move on while still licking my wounds and trying my best to heal? No. She opened up my wounds with her mess and they were fresh. She taunted me with phone calls from his house. She told me that she was married to him and was pregnant. She told me that she had already moved into Floyd's house—the same house that Floyd and I had shared.

Rhonda started calling me on a regular basis. I guess she was trying to find out whether I was still involved with Floyd. Floyd was my ex-fiancé. We had been together for five years—living together and working together. I suppose she got my number from his caller I.D. Like I said, I knew of her. I knew she and Floyd had a relationship. I also knew that Floyd and I were still involved. We were even going to counseling to see if we might still work things out.

Again, she started all the craziness, not that I needed her to start craziness in my life. I was already having an affair with another married man with whom Floyd and I both worked. I had been lying to Floyd for nearly two years about that. That was the main reason why our relationship failed. He lost trust in me. I guess I should also mention that I did end up sleeping with my old college boyfriend, Thomas. His wife ended up calling me in the middle of the night yelling and screaming at me, wanting to know if I was the same woman that Thomas had dated in college before she married him. Anyway, I digress. Eventually, Rhonda and I started harassing each other by telephone, calling each other the most derogatory names we could think of, saying the most hurtful, vile things that we could make up. Now, understand, she was an executive working for a major corporation, and I was a Family Counselor, so we both were educated, successful, attractive women.

One day, I decided to stop by Floyd's house and check on him because one of our co-workers had said that he had been out sick. Normally, Floyd and I would talk several times daily. Though no longer together, we were still very good friends. When I arrived at the house, I saw Rhonda's silver Lexus sitting in the driveway. I immediately began fuming. Don't ask me why I did what I did next. I rang the doorbell, knowing he would not answer it. After that, I went to the garage door, which I knew would be open, and just burst in through the kitchen. There she sat, at MY kitchen table. They looked as if they were getting ready to go out. Floyd immediately corralled me back outside while I yelled, spitted insults, and tried to scratch my way past him. After he got me out of the house, I did the typical "pissed-off ex-girlfriend" move. I keyed his car. Well, let's just say, after the police came and towed my car (for driving with a suspended license due to unpaid speeding tickets) and politely escorted me to the jail where I had to wait for my best friend to come pick me up and take me to sneak my car out of tow, I had no other choice except to give up.

Believe it or not, the silliness went on, and on, and on for several more weeks. It finally took a week long trip to D.C. to get away from it all. In the end, I changed my number and my mind about being with Floyd."

Denise M., 31

CHAPTER 4

Thicker Than Water

As young girls, we learn to prepare ourselves for marriage and children. We're taught to cook well in order to feed and nourish our husbands and families. We learn how to care for our homes so that we can make their lives comfortable. We learn to take care of ourselves so that our husbands continue to desire us and we learn to be supportive and loving "in sickness and in health." What we don't learn is what we should do when all this preparation fails to do that which it is supposed to—keep our man happy and at home. Even more, what we don't learn is what we should do when our unhappy man finds happiness in the arms of one of our best friends or family members.

When those whom we embrace as family betray us in such a manner, we begin to question the very meaning of love. Because we often define ourselves through the relationships we share with those close to us, surviving this betrayal of trust is nearly an impossible task. When friendship and family somehow become synonymous with pain, we are left wondering what we did that deserved punishment. And, unfortunately, because we are often blamed by our betrayers for their transgressions, we are left agonizing over our faults. We are also left wondering why we failed to recognize the signs that are now so clear, and how we could have ever placed our trust in people who never deserved it in the first place.

It is doubtful that even the woman herself could really explain why she chose to ignore the bonds of your relationship and pursue a man who was obviously off limits. Of all the men on earth, why would she choose your husband? Your boyfriend? Most often, the excuse is simply, "It just happened." Followed by, "We never intended to hurt anyone." And finally, "I'm sorry." The most heartless of women will even continue to pursue your husband after you have separated from him.

When remembering those things that we have been taught, stealing your girlfriend's man was not one of them, nor was sleeping with your sister's husband, or kissing your mother's lover. So, what do you do when it happens? Do you rant and rave and kick your friend's ass? Or, do you crawl under your bed and as the song says, "roll up into a big old ball and die"? The answer is, "none of the above." What you do is move on, and you don't let this failure dictate the way in which you live the rest of your life. Life can be hard, and there will be disappointments, but one thing we were taught was to always, no matter what life may bring, stay strong, hold your head high, and always do the right thing, no matter what someone has done to you.

❦   ❦   ❦

Scenario:

Christy is a partner in a family business, along with her mother and two cousins. Her mother's ex-boyfriend, Todd, is a manager for one of the companies with whom they do business. Christy develops a friendship with Todd that soon turns romantic. Throughout their courtship, Todd speaks negatively about Christy's mother and the relationship they had. Christy adds her two cents, mom finds out, all friendships are severed and the trust is ruined between mother and daughter.

Code #46:

Never become intimate with any man with whom your mother has ever been involved. **This includes anyone with whom she has held hands, met for dinner dates, kissed etc.**

Code #47:

Never engage in mom-bashing with anyone, let alone a man who first slept with your mother and is now trying to sleep with you. Elevating one woman above another is a common ploy men use when attempting to make the "new" woman feel more desired by them. Considering that the other woman in this case is Christy's mom, this situation is even more disgusting.

Girlfriend 911: The first time a man talks negatively about your mother you should turn the tables and start bashing *him.* Then, tell him to kiss your ass as you walk proudly out of the door.

Scenario:

Bobby and Imani are very happily married. Imani openly shares the wonderful things about her husband with her family. Imani's sister, Denise, is jealous of their relationship and takes every opportunity to criticize Bobby to Imani and other members of the family.

Code # 48:

Never allow jealousy to get in the way of your relationship with your girlfriend/sister and her happiness.

Girlfriend 911: Jealously is a natural emotion, and all of us experience this feeling at some time or another. But,

when your girlfriend or sister is genuinely happy, find it in your heart to be happy for her also, and pray that she remains that way.

Scenario:

Debra was Ladonna's matron of honor at her wedding. She is the godmother of Ladonna's children and has often been in the company of Ladonna's husband. When Ladonna and her husband separate, Debra makes herself readily available to help Ladonna's husband out with the children. As a result, they become closer and eventually become lovers. In time, he pops the question.

Code #49:

Never marry your girlfriend's ex-husband.
   Girlfriend 911: No comment

Scenario:

Debra has been dating Duane for 6 months. She is 35 years old and feels her biological time clock slowing to a crawl. Duane invites her to accompany him to Thanksgiving dinner at his family's home, where Debra meets and "befriends" Duane's mother. For months following Thanksgiving, Debra is in constant contact with Duane's mother, going to lunch, shopping, movies etc. Duane's mother encourages him to marry Debra. After the wedding, Debra no longer calls Duane's mother.

Code #50:

Never befriend a man's family with the sole purpose of eventually hooking up with him romantically. **If your man's family was influential enough in his decision-making to contribute to you two getting together, wouldn't it be reasonable to think that they could now influence him to dump you too? Those that use others simply to get what they want, usually wind up getting what they deserve.**

Scenario:

Yvette bumped into Griselda's college boyfriend while out shopping. They exchange numbers and develop a friendship over the telephone. Yvette soon realizes that she wants to take the relationship to another level. She eventually calls Griselda and tells her about her feelings for her ex-boyfriend and asks her permission to pursue the relationship further.

Code # 51:

Never think it's okay to ask permission to date your girl-friend's ex. First of all, the mere fact that you feel the need to ask permission should be the red, waving flag that screams for you NOT to do something. Permission does not equal approval. If by chance you receive a "yes" from your girlfriend, don't assume it is a sincere "yes." It may be a "Girl, get out of my face with that shit, yes" or a "Girl, do whatever you want, yes." Either way, be smart and find someone who has not been intimate with one of your friends.

Breaking the Code
No Longer My Sister

"We had been friends since we were young girls playing hopscotch, double-dutch and jacks in front of whomever's house we happened to be visiting that day. It didn't matter whose house it was though. All that mattered for us was that we were hanging together, and for me, time spent without Lynn and Renee was time spent looking forward to our next game of jacks. So, as you can see, we were not just friends, we were sisters. This is why it brought such agonizing devastation to learn that Renee, my sister, had tried to seduce my husband in my own home.

I was having a cookout and had, as usual, invited my girls. Lynn, the third Musketeer, was out of the country and couldn't be there, so it didn't surprise me even when Lynn called that evening following the cookout. What did surprise me were the words she revealed that night. She had just received an emotional phone call from Renee, who was supposedly distraught because of something she had done. According to her, she had followed my husband into the dimly lit basement of my home and proceeded to remove her shirt, baring her breasts. My husband failed to acknowledge her at all, retrieved the extra containers of juice he had gone to the basement for, and returned upstairs to me. What she didn't know was that my husband, in all his sweetness, was oblivious to her futile attempt at seduction. So, the very thing that had caused her guilt was what she had perceived as rejection. She moaned and groaned to Lynn about how sorrowful she felt for her behavior. She even blamed her lack of judgment on intoxication, though there was no alcohol served at my cookout. She finally admitted to being jealous of me and my happiness, and reasoned that her unforgivable behavior was her way of lashing out. She pleaded to Lynn for forgiveness and to intercede on her behalf, but with that one act, on that one night, our sisterhood ceased to exist. And that fact alone caused me unbearable pain. Knowing that someone I loved so dearly, and wished only goodness, could possess the hatred of a stranger was unfathomable.

Initially, she tried to contact me. I assume she wanted to apologize, but I had no desire to hear her voice utter even one sound. On that day, Renee died, and Lynn and I have remained embraced in our sisterhood without her."

Janet B., 43

Breaking the Code
The Sounds of Deception

"I walked in the door, and from my back bedroom I could hear sounds, quite familiar, but without my involvement. As she moaned and asked for more, her voice was quite distinctive. I knew who she was. When I heard my husband's voice, the reality hit me like a brick. I couldn't take another step. I wasn't able to go any further into the house; all I could do was make a pitiful attempt at breathing. Even that seemed impossible. Then I thought of my children. Where were my children? Were they at one of the neighbor's? At the park? Or, were they just sent somewhere to play? I got myself together and decided to slam the door as hard as I could, hoping it would interrupt the sound of their fucking. It did. After gathering myself and finding my children, I knew that I had to get myself together. I had just witnessed my husband and my best friend fucking for longer than I care to remember. I moved into an apartment with my children the very next day feeling hurt, deceived, mistreated, and discarded by both my husband and my best friend of 5 years."

Sakile M., 56

Breaking the Code
Pillow Talk

"I was introduced to my first love, Troy, by my girlfriend, Yvonne, during my junior year in high school. Yvonne and I attended the same university and remained very close during the first two years of college. She became pregnant during that second year and married Boyd, Troy's best friend. Boyd and Yvonne eventually separated, around the same time Troy and I broke off our relationship. While we all remained as friends, I soon found out from Troy that he and Yvonne had been lovers during the entire time she was married. He told me that she would compare herself to me, and ask questions of him that suggested that he do the same. She also divulged all of the secrets, good and bad, that I had shared with her over the years concerning my relationship with him."

Leslie S., 22

CHAPTER 5

In His Eyes

As women, we are quick to have a male-bashing party, but instead of beating up on the men in our lives, we should point our fingers at ourselves. We spend hours screaming about how awful men are. We call men dogs. We call men trifling and no good, but we fail to call ourselves the names we should. How can we have these conversations about men when we, ourselves, are undermining our own relationships? When we allow ourselves to be a part of an affair, we are just as wrong as the man with whom we are involved. We believe that we are a prize, that we have earned some honor, that we have won out on some competition that makes us better than the woman we screwed in order to screw her man. But, what we have really earned is the title of home wrecker. When we chase a man who doesn't want to be chased, we are stalkers. And when we lie to our friend to hook up with her man, we can't be trusted. Plain and simple.

We have been described by men as being like sharks after fresh meat, acting as if life depends on having a man. Would we describe this behavior as good? It would be best described using all of the adjectives we use to describe men—trifling, no good, and dishonest. So, instead of crying that there are no good men left in the world, let's take a look in the mirror first. Maybe then we can spend the rest of our time getting ourselves together, rather than wasting it complaining about men.

"As a male, I have come to deeply appreciate that God proceeded to make woman after making man. With my appreciation, comes a sincere admiration for how different men and women are from each other. I admire the sensitive and nurturing qualities with which women are generally blessed. I admire their ability to love in a manner that is superior to that of men. This includes the relationship that women share with each other. When positive, I have observed the best in relationships between women regardless of the origin. I have experienced two who are not related grow into sisterhood and a mother-in-law/daughter-in-law transform into a relationship as mother and daughter. When negative, I have seen sisters behave as if they are the strongest of enemies. There is no match to the strength of bond that can exist between women. Conversely, men seldom engage in the conniving and devious behavior that women may often display towards each other. Their virtuous ability to love can be polar opposite to their potential, disdainful behavior."

Phillip A., 38; Investment Analyst; Georgia; Single

"I had an affair with a woman from church. We spent a lot of time together. She even shopped for my child and for the house I shared with my wife and daughter. On several occasions she even paid a bill or two for me. After two years of this, I wanted to get out of it. At first, she acted as if she understood my decision. But after a while, she started driv-

ing by my house, stopping by my job, and trying to get my friends to talk to me about getting back with her. When this didn't work, she started harassing my wife. She left messages at the house telling about things we had done together. She even went to my daughter's school claiming she just wanted to say hello to her."
Joseph M.; 24; Law Clerk; Illinois; Divorced

"At the time, I was a Human Resource Manager and eventually developed a serious, but uncommitted relationship with a co-worker. After a while, she moved to Atlanta, and married. We stayed in touch, and would, despite her marriage, get together occasionally. She started working for a human resources company in Atlanta and communicated details about our relationship to the other women on her team. Soon, one of the other women called me and suggested that we hook up for a date. She actually said, "I know you're coming to see Felecia, but if you don't mind, I'd like to hook up." I declined. One day, out of the blue, I went to the job to surprise Felecia. When she came to the lobby to meet me, a few of the other women came with her. This made the other woman, Felecia's boss, want to hook up with me even more. I ended up hooking up with the boss sexually without Felecia's knowledge. But then, the boss started becoming possessive. She even called me in Felecia's presence. Felecia overheard the conversation, and confronted her, which became physical. This situation

destroyed the relationship between them and ruined the morale on that team."
Pierre L., 36; Mortgage Broker; Tennessee; Single

"My neighbor called asking me to come over and help her change a flat tire. I told her that I was out of town and couldn't help her. She wanted to know whether I was with a girl. I laughed it off and told her I was out of town on business, which was true. She later called stating that the "girl I was with" had called her from my cell phone asking her who she was and why she was calling my cell phone. She even went so far as to tell me that I needed to get my girlfriend in check. It was hilarious because I knew that she was lying. I was actually with two male co-workers. I knew immediately that this was a case of a woman trying to cause chaos, and I avoided her from that point on."
Derrick B., 42; Police Officer; Georgia; Divorced

"I'll never forget being greeted at the door of my mother in law's house by the gatekeepers, my mother-in-law and father-in-law, standing there guarding their daughter from me, her husband. Now, I could understand if there was any abuse. By all means, keep me away from your child. But, that was not the case. We had simply argued, and my wife had gone over there out of anger. This was not the only time that my mother-in-law has interfered in our relationship. This woman even tried to keep me out of the delivery

room when my daughter was born. She has instigated conflicts, and has coerced my wife into going against my wishes. It's almost as if she doesn't want our marriage to succeed. I've never understood it."
Johnny G., 20; Dancer; Washington, D.C; Married

"When I was 15 years old, I was taken in by Mr. and Mrs. Preston, a prestigious couple living in Georgia. They were my unofficial, adopted parents—my Mom and Dad. Even though I now had a comfortable life, I still didn't get serious about my schooling. Because of this, I was twenty-one before I graduated from high school. By this time, Mom had moved to New Orleans with her kids and I soon followed. I was very excited to get my first real job and I began to meet a lot of people. Soon, I met a very attractive older woman who was eager to spend time with me romantically. Out of respect though, I would only invite her to our house when Mom wasn't home. There were many times when she overheard conversations between Mom and me. She began to listen to the phone calls and question why I allowed her to tell me what to do. Her opinion was that I was a grown man and should not allow Mom to control any aspect of my life. She even wrote out a plan for me to move out of Mom's house. At this point, she still hadn't met Mom. Once she met Mom at church one Sunday, her attitude worsened. Because mom is very attractive and really looks younger than her age, she began to question the nature of our rela-

tionship. She suggested that we were probably having sex and if not, we soon would be. Her interference and negative comments were constant and affected my relationship with Mom. I listened to what she was saying and felt justified in being disrespectful sometimes. It wasn't until an older friend intervened that I came back to my senses and left that woman alone."
Richard S., 23; Student; New Orleans; Single

"While serving time in jail, I felt it selfish that I maintain a relationship with my girlfriend, Quanisha. I told her that she was free to date and do her own thing, but with the understanding that we would get back together when I got out. When I was released, we got back together and started our relationship over. It was difficult though, and we argued often. After one of our blowouts, I invited another girl to a concert. The other girl knew I had a girlfriend, but for a long time had been trying to hook up with me anyway. Everything was cool until Quanisha showed up with her girls ready to beat my ass and the girl's too."
Wright J., 18; Dance Teacher; Georgia; Married

"Every woman wants a man. Though women may or may not want a particular man, they often want the security that having a man—*any man*—provides. Because of many reasons, some women may not care if that man is taken. Jealousy plays a role, as does competitiveness and insecurity. Sometimes being able to attract another woman's man brings additional fulfillment and validation. Sometimes it's just a lack of self-control and discipline. Men respect women more when they do the right thing. When women give in to our junk we lose respect for them."

Shon J., 43; Health Care; Tennessee; Married

Conclusion:

The Universal Clit

Life is imperfect and, as humans, so are we. Consequently, it is a given that we will frequently choose the wrong path on which to travel. Often, we will unintentionally make choices that bring pain to those within our reach. But, because women are innately equipped with the tools needed to discern what is considered emotionally healthy from that which is considered emotionally unhealthy, we must be more diligent in resisting the urge to possess the "by any means necessary approach" when looking for romance. Though we empathize with the feelings of other women, we often ignore those feelings in pursuit of self gratification. These are the times when life is the most challenging for us. These are also the times when we are forced to look within ourselves and take a stance—will we bend to the temptations of the flesh or will we stand strong and proud, refusing to bow in the face of these trials?

As women, we have a particularly crucial role in maintaining a balance between "the good" and "not so good" role of the men in our lives. Our steadfastness protects the institution of marriage, which, in turn, protects the family. Therefore, we cannot allow the desire to "get a man" weaken our moral fiber, nor allow this desire to dictate how we live our lives—to encourage us to do the very thing we would not want done to us. As women, it is important for us to come to grips with the fact that when we go searching for a man, what most of us really desire is the love and companionship that a man may provide. What we are looking for is LOVE. Unfortunately, this search for love can, in the process, translate into vindictiveness, game-playing, backstabbing, lying and desperation instead of the security for which we are really grasping. Wanting love is not a bad thing. Stabbing another woman in the back to get it is another story.

Yes, life is imperfect, but this does not mean that we aren't blessed with the power to choose to be a help rather than a hindrance to our girlfriends and those girlfriends we have yet to meet. For, within a girlfriend—girlfriend relationship lies the automatic assumption that loyalty is the binding force of that relationship. This is the concept on which the Universal Clit is based. We are one. Hence, there are never any second thoughts, nor any regrets. We are invited into the intimate world of women and entrusted with each other's husbands, boyfriends, children, lives. Girlfriends are there to shop until we drop and gossip over platters of hot wings and pitchers of margaritas. We hold each other's hands during break-ups, childbirths, miscarriages and calamities at work. And, we hold in our hands the power to keep drama at bay. This is why we, as girlfriends, must not ignore the responsibility of that entitlement. There is a price to pay for doing anything other than this. Those women who choose to do the right thing and follow a moral code will always have each other's backs and be a support system in one another's lives. But, those who choose to ignore that code risk living a life of isolation and disillusion. And, no matter how hard you try to convince yourselves that there is nothing wrong with living a life holding the hand of another woman's man, you are mistaken. Otherwise, why is there a need for secrecy? Why is it really not okay to call this man at home? No matter how hard you try, then, to convince yourself that what you've done is right, you know it wasn't cool. So, let's not have this conversation again. Okay?

The Girlfriend's Commandments

1. *Thou shall always have your girlfriend's back. You are your sister's keeper.*

2. *Thou shall respect each other at all times.*

3. *Thou shall always keep confidential those things your girlfriend tells you.*

4. *Thou shall always try to lend an ear to your girlfriend when she needs a confidant.*

5. *Thou shall always be willing to share information with your girlfriend that can allow her be successful and secure.*

6. *Thou shall always be an upbeat and positive influence in your girlfriend's life.*

7. *Thou shall always be willing to forgive your girlfriend.*

8. *Thou shall always pray for one another.*

9. *Thou shall grow together in love and have a purposeful life.*

10. *Thou shall always be honest with your girlfriend.*

11. *Thou shall always stay true to the "Girlfriend's Code of Ethics" … and stand for what is right.*

The Girlfriend's Code of Ethics Survey

Self-Examination Survey

Part I

Check all that apply:

I am:

a. between the ages of: ___ 15–25 ___ 26–35 ___ 36–45
   ___ 46–55 ___ over 55

b. ___ married ___ single, never married ___ engaged
   ___ divorced ___ widowed

c. ___ African-Am. ___ White ___ Asian ___ Hispanic
   ___ Native American ___ Other

d. currently residing in the:　　___ South ___ Southeast
   　　　　　　　　　　　　　　___ Southwest ___ Midwest
   　　　　　　　　　　　　　　___ Northeast ___ Northwest
   　　　　　　　　　　　　　　___ Other

e. ___ currently employed ___ currently unemployed ___ a student

Part II

Instructions: For each item, please circle a number in the right column to show the degree to which the item describes your behavior.
Scale:

1= never, 2=rarely, 3=sometimes, 4=often, 5=always

1. I have considered having an affair with my friend's husband or boyfriend.   1 2 3 4 5

2. I have had an affair with a married man.   1 2 3 4 5

3. I have been involved with a man who was already in a relationship.   1 2 3 4 5

4. I have deliberately caused problems in a friend's relationship.   1 2 3 4 5

5. I encourage other women to maintain sexual relationships with married men.   1 2 3 4 5

6. I have used alcohol as an excuse for bad behavior.   1 2 3 4 5

7. If I hurt someone, I think my apology is sufficient enough to excuse the behavior.   1 2 3 4 5

8. I have communicated with my girlfriend's husband or boyfriend without her knowledge.   1 2 3 4 5

9. I have contacted the wife or girlfriend of the man with whom I was having an affair.   1 2 3 4 5

10. I feel no sense of obligation to women whom I don't know.   1 2 3 4 5

11.   I have accused a woman who I believed was hav-   1 2 3 4 5
       ing an affair with my husband or boyfriend.

12.   I am suspicious of another woman's intent   1 2 3 4 5
       towards my husband or boyfriend.

13.   Other women can trust me with their husband or   1 2 3 4 5
       boyfriend.

14.   I continue to have a sexual relationship with my   1 2 3 4 5
       now married or otherwise committed ex-boyfriend
       or ex-husband.

15.   I feel victorious when I am successful in ending   1 2 3 4 5
       another woman's relationship.

Part III

Instructions: Read the statement. Then, for each pair of words, mark the point closest to your belief.

16.   There are enough men in the world to go around.

       True ____ ____ ____ ____ ____ ____ ____ False
              1   2   3   4   5   6   7

17.   I believe that I can trust my best friend with someone who I am dat-
       ing.

       True ____ ____ ____ ____ ____ ____ ____ False
              1   2   3   4   5   6   7

18.   Women are not ruthless when it comes to getting a man.

       True ____ ____ ____ ____ ____ ____ ____ False
              1   2   3   4   5   6   7

19.   I believe that all men are faithful and honest.

True ____ ____ ____ ____ ____ ____ ____ False
     1   2   3   4   5   6   7

20. I believe people should be held accountable for their actions.

True ____ ____ ____ ____ ____ ____ ____ False
     1   2   3   4   5   6   7

Now that you've completed the survey, total your scores for all of the questions in each category. Using the chart below, find out where you fall in the Girlfriend's Code of Ethics self examination survey. Then, log on to www.girlfriendscode.com to enter your scores and compare them to the scores of other people who've recently taken our survey.

Score: If your score fell between 20 and 40:

Congratulations and keep up the good work! You are already the type of girlfriend other women can trust with their significant other. You seem to respect and appreciate committed relationships, as well as yourself. You believe that people are good, but should be held accountable for their actions. You make good choices and seem to be a girlfriend who tries to encourage others to do the right thing at all times. More women should try to live the way that you do.

Score: If your score fell between 41 and 100:

You seem to be on the fence when it comes to respecting the boundaries of a committed relationship. For example, you may not choose to have an affair with your best friend's man, but you may see nothing wrong with carrying on with the husband or boyfriend of a woman whom you don't know. You may also make excuses for bad behavior, blaming your actions on intoxication or moodiness, rather than faulty decision-making. Correcting this behavior is simply a matter of altering your way of thinking about things. In other words, know and believe that there is a better way of living your life.

Score: If your score was 101 or above:

You need help and shouldn't be left alone with any man that is already in a relationship. You have no respect for relationships, whether that relationship is between a woman and her man or between you and your girlfriends. You are probably one who makes excuses for your actions, and expects an apology for wrongdoing to be a sufficient remedy. Because you don't really believe in the goodness of other people, you don't believe that you are good and deserving of good things either. Your actions, therefore, reflect this belief. Despite this, it is never too late to change.

978-0-595-45783-0
0-595-45783-5